Acknowledgments

This book is dedicated in the memory of my dad, who opened my eyes to free-roaming rabbits! To my wonderful mother who inspires me with her comedic ways. My mother was a force in writing this story; her input did not go unnoticed.

This book is also dedicated to Varun Soti, all of my family and friends who support my dreams. You know who you are! And last, thank you to the fire rescue team that volunteered their time to catch Able.

About Me

Sonja Hall appeared on the Dean's list (of FIU) and graduated from Florida International University with a Bachelor of Arts degree. She later went on to writing poetry and pursued animal photography as one of her passions.

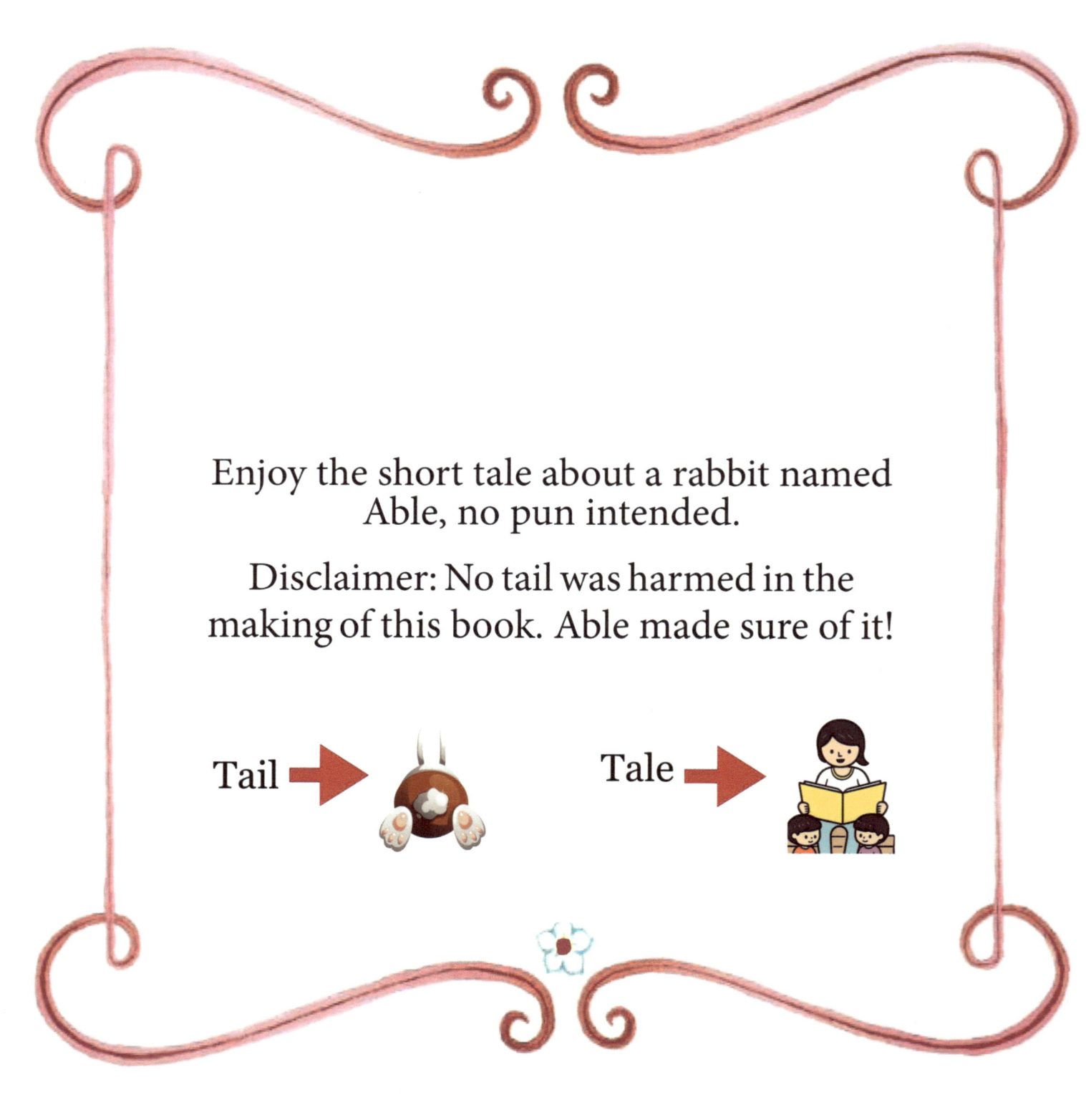

Enjoy the short tale about a rabbit named Able, no pun intended.

Disclaimer: No tail was harmed in the making of this book. Able made sure of it!

Tail ➡️ 🐇   Tale ➡️ 👩‍👧‍👦

Copyright 2024 © by Sonja Hall

All rights reserved. Published in the United States.

No part of this book may be reproduced or transmitted in any form or by any means, electronic or mechanical, including photocopying, recording, or by any information storage and retrieval system, without written consent from the author.

August 2024

ISBN 979-8-9912558-3-7

Today is Saturday, October 21, 2023, and my owner has been trying to catch me. You see, I am her pet rabbit. I'm a fast runner and know how to hide. I hear when she comes because I have tall ears like an antenna to hear from far away. I'm always on the lookout for predators, and I always keep my eyes open. As I roam, I eat a lot of new plants: some are great, but others are frightening; however, I like to experiment! My mother warned me about the temptation of poisonous flowers. Hard to resist with the sweet aroma and inviting texture, but I am glad I listened.

I like to stay out all night and make my owner look for me. I could see her coming and hear her calling my name repeatedly. Able! I didn't tell my mom I was heading out of the yard and into the wild because I knew she would forewarn me of all the dangers in the wooded areas. My mom still thinks I am a baby, but at the ripe age of 3 years old (rabbit years), I am ready to explore the unknown and venture out. See the world behind this fence. I am Able. Are you able?

I see more bumblebees out here along my path to what I believe is freedom. I enjoy the unknown, but it's scary out here because there are wild animals, such as raccoons, possums, and wild dogs. I do not see them, but I smell them, so I know that they are nearby.

While I explore behind the back fence where I'm now living, I hear Ally (our family dog) bark like an alarm going off to my owner to tell my current location like coordinates. Beep beep. SOS. I now hear leaves crunching under my owner's feet. My owner calls out Able Able. I then bolt back under the neighbor's fence, and under the wooden deck, I go.

Late night in the wee hours, I dig dig. I wiggle wiggle. I dig my way through the bottom of the fence and sneak back into my backyard. While my owner is asleep inside her house, I see that all the lights are off in the house. It's pitch black, with no noise from inside, only the crickets cricking, the birds chirping, ribbits and bees humming in my location. Yum, mmm, my owner left some food out for me; it's carrots!!

If I want more carrots, I will have to risk my life and travel 1 mile out through the wilderness to get carrots in Alexis's Garden. Alexis lives within a good hopping distance, and she started her very own garden lined with thyme, carrots and lavender. I can smell the aroma of fresh thyme – Mamma Mia, I also like the scent.

It's a full moon out tonight. Fireflies start to dance through the night. While the bees go back to their hives, I noticed the crickets are laying low. I don't hear the frogs anymore. It seems everyone is in hiding. What I do hear is drumbeats. Somebody's beating on a drum. Must be a neighbor beating on the drum. I spot a coyote nearby that glowed in front of the full moon. I hide deep in the bushes, hoping he does not smell me. This is when I discover I need my home!! I want to go to my safe haven. I don't want to be somebody's lunch. My owner, my mother and my siblings await me. This is when I see for the first time I'm all alone in this wilderness without the protection of the family dog, my owner and my mom. They are my village. The spotlight is on me now, and not in a good way. Oh wait, that's just in my head. I will stay calm, venture back behind the fence and under the wooden deck I go, into my hiding place.

"A fad back in the 80's"

~ 15 ~

This is when I fall asleep. And I dream that my tail was cut off and that my tail was stolen, and it became a fad. My bunny tail collected on all the key rings as good luck. What was that about? What did that dream mean?

Anyway, it's 6:45 PM, and I hear my owner calling out my name. I hear my owner calling out, "Able, Able," and then I hear footsteps coming towards me. And suddenly, a loud sound, "BAM BAM" knocks on top of the wooden deck, and I look out and see that I am surrounded by my owner and 3 other people at each corner. One person even had a net to catch me. I did what I do best, and I darted out of there and flew up into the air and kicked my legs high. I move at lightning speed and will catch everyone by surprise at how fast I run around. I had them in circles, running back and forth. "Hmmm, time to think outside the box." That is when I moved back into my hiding place under the neighbor's wooden deck but this time I am beside the peep hole. It feels like I've been out on my own for years, but it's only been 2 and 1/2 weeks. They all gave up on catching me. One by one, I hear their footsteps go in the opposite direction as I stayed still under the deck, watching them go.

The noise of the cars sounds louder out here, vroom vroom. I am now out of my hiding place and have positioned myself on the sidewalk right between my owner's house and her neighbor. I am hiding in the trees that align the sidewalk. I see people walk by with their dogs, and a little boy points out, "Look, I see a rabbit." The mother stops walking and says, "yes! you are right, there is a brown rabbit with a white stripe on his shoulder." Then they walk closer towards me, and I jump away from them into the wooded area.

I then return to the same location along the sidewalk, and then suddenly, I see my owner walking with our family dog, Ally. Then Ally moves her nose in my direction, and I am spotted. This time, my owner did not come after me. She must have given up on catching me. I will hang out here a little longer. Well, that will be a first. I saw her walking away to go back to her house. Little did I know that my owner had gone to the local fire department with a frightening story about "me" running away into the wild. She has shared details about the possum and raccoon she saw (it must have been the same one I smelled the other day). So, the fire department was persuaded to come to my house. Geez, I cannot get a break.

I am now in my front yard, camouflaged under the small palm tree. I blended right in with the brown rocks. As I sat under the baby coconut palm tree with its yellow palm that touched my back, I watched my owner drive up into her driveway with a big red truck right behind her. The truck must have been 40 feet long! It had large hoses at the sides. What is that thing doing here? Four men came out from the red truck with heavy-duty gloves. That is when I saw 2 of them approach me. Little by little, they got closer, and then when they lunged at me, I ran into the backyard (on the side of the house). My owner came to the side of the backyard yelling there he is, and I ran between 2 of their legs, and then I was finally caught by a giant of a man.

"Look, I caught him." I wiggled to get out of his hand, but I could not wiggle my way out. I was caught. My owner then thanked him, and she was smiling from ear to ear.

I am back in the cage now, but my owner lets me out from time to time. My time out of the cage is more restricted and now I have to be watched by my owner when I am out running around in the backyard.

She loves to watch me run back and forth. Jump in the air while I kick my feet. I see her face change whenever I do that. So I do that often, and yes, I am showing off! Wee wee! Across the field, I go. So fast I almost fly as I kick my feet and go from side to side, which causes my owner to move her head from side to side.

"The hills are alive with the sound of music!" I found a mound to hop over. My owner is about to plant a tree. I can do this all day.

"Humor me," I think in my head. My owner has blocked off all corners of the fence from row to row. Ha-ha-ha. She is trying to prevent my next escape. I dig, and I dig, but I cannot escape. I dig when she turns her head, and the dirt flies between my feet. "Able! Able" Stop it. I freeze! I freeze! I pose. "Stop digging," my owner repeats.

I am fresh. I am clean. I wipe, wipe and wipe my feet with my tongue from top to bottom. Grooming is my thing. I love to stay clean. I am fresh. I stay still. As my owner rushes over to me, I bolt across the yard and hide behind her banana tree. Then I start eating the banana flowers that fall to the ground.

So, it has been years now that I have lived in the backyard with my mother and siblings. We are a close-knit family except for my brother Angel. (I am glad my owner did not name him Cain) We are rivals by nature, but it was not always that way. We were close initially when we were babies, but nature has it we would become rivals. You see, we will fight if we are both out of the cage at the same time, so we have to take turns going outside of our cage.

I cannot complain. I am older now, and I see the care given to me. I am fed, loved and taken care of. I do not have to forage for food. I no longer have the fear that I had when I was out in the wilderness. I look forward to more hay, please, and clean water. I'm good. I love it here now. This is when I found out that my owner had prayed for me while I was out in the wild. My owner prayed for me to come home safely. My mother (Ellen, AKA Allen) patiently waited each day for me to return. I am more mature now, and I appreciate my life, my home, my village, my owner and family. Even the family dog, Ally, my protector. I understand now what life is beyond the fence.

The End.

Reading Comprehension Questions

How does Able escape?

What is Able's favorite food that he finds outside?

What does Able dream about one night?

What is the name of Able's brother?

What noise did Able hear while the full moon was out?

How many fire men came out of the fire truck (red – fire truck)?

Where was Able hiding when the fire men first arrived?

What is the name of Able's protector?

How far does Able have to travel to get carrots?

What did Able learn in the end?

In the picture, from left to right, are: Abby, Allen, Ally (Protector), Angel, and Able (main character)

Dear Readers,

    I am grateful to you for taking the time to hop on the adventure into **Able and the Great Escape**. As an author, your support doesn't go unrecognized. Please rate this book online and leave a review. Whether it's a few words about the story, what you like or how it made you feel. Your review is of value and appreciated!

There is an underlying message in my story; of which, I feel compelled to share and that is the best things in life are free - the love in our hearts. As adults, sometimes we can forget those simple truths.

Sonja Hall

www.ingramcontent.com/pod-product-compliance
Lightning Source LLC
Chambersburg PA
CBHW040723060526
44119CB00083B/303